CW01507864

Tongues of Fire

- 12 Reasons for Speaking in Tongues
- The Historical Basis for Tongues
- … and more

Matthew Ashimolowo

Mattyson Media

Mattyson Media Company
57 Maryland Road
Stratford
London E15 1JL

ISBN: 1–874646–03–1

Typeset by CRB (Drayton) Typesetting Services, Norwich
Printed in England by Clays Ltd, St Ives plc

Contents

Acknowledgements

There comes a time in our life, when we need the love and affirming of others, to fulfil God's mandate on our life.

This book is dedicated to all those Eagle Believers, who make up Kingsway International Christian Centre, London. They have what it takes to make a vision come true.

God will not forget them.

Introduction

The time was 5.00 pm. I was in the process of packing in readiness for my journey back to Britain from Nigeria. My friend, an executive in one of the local banks in Lagos, called me on the phone to say she was on her way to see me. As soon as she came in she introduced the purpose of her visit. She wanted to receive the gifts of the Holy Spirit.

According to her she had seen the difference the Holy Spirit makes in the life and the ministry of believers, that is, people who allow the Holy Spirit to live in them. There was a problem; while my friend desired this gift she did not want to speak in tongues! Her objections to this experience made me curious, so I asked for her reasons.

Her first reason for objecting was because she had heard of people speaking in what she considered counterfeit tongues, and she did not want any of that. She had also been in the company of people who objected to the teaching of tongues as a benefit available to all believers and as an initial evidence of being baptised in the Holy Spirit. They were of the opinion that speaking in tongues was for few people only, and also optional.

I could not think of a better way of helping her realise that they come in 'the same package' and it was a benefit she should not miss.

I went into detailed reasons why she should speak in tongues and explained why we need to speak in tongues regularly.

Chapter 1

12 Reasons Why You Should Speak in Tongues Regularly

1. Edification

> *'He that speaketh in an unknown tongue edifieth himself.'*　　　(1 Corinthians 14:4a)

Speaking in tongues has a wonderful effect of building up our spirit. The word 'edify' comes from the Greek word *'oikodome'* and in the context in which it was used in the scripture passage above it suggests an action which results in growth or building oneself up.

Before we were reconciled to God, the state of our human spirit was literally 'death', or rather rendered inactive by sin. When we become born again, our spirit comes alive, but like the carnal or non-growing Christian we are dominated by our five senses.

The senses of touch, taste, smell, sight, and hearing still have a profound effect on our faith. Our capacity to perceive and respond to spiritual things is limited by our senses. Speaking in tongues therefore helps our spirit to grow to effectively perceive the things of God.

Edification is one of the purposes of speaking in tongues, in private or public use.

> *'But ye, beloved, building up yourselves on your most holy faith, praying in the Holy Ghost keep yourselves in the love of God.'*
>
> (Jude 20–21)

As the believer engages in speaking every day, something beyond ordinary language is going on. Consequently the fruit of the spirit starts to replace the works of the flesh.

The two are contrasted in Paul's book to the Galatians:

> *'Now the works of the flesh are manifest which are these; Adultery, fornication, uncleanness, lasciviousness, idolatry, witchcraft, hatred, variance, emulations, wrath, strife, seditions, heresies, Envyings, murders, drunkenness, revellings, and such like: of the which I tell you before, as I have also told you in time past, that they which do such things shall not inherit the kingdom of God. But the fruit of the Spirit is*

> *love, joy, peace, longsuffering, gentleness, goodness, faith. Meekness, temperance, against such, there is no law.'* (Galatians 5:19–23)

An edified spirit in the believer will help him respond to spiritual things. The human spirit will be groomed to maturity.

2. Declaration of Mysteries

Speaking in tongues ushers the speaker into declaring the great and deep mysteries of the kingdom of God. This brings into the open things that are otherwise unnoticed and unknown. Declaring mysteries through tongues will make you grow in spiritual things. You would be able to stand like King Saul *'shoulders high above your brethren'*. Praying in tongues will make *'the deep call unto the deep at the sound of the water spouts'*.

As you speak in tongues you bring to the consciousness of your spirit things hidden from the wise which are only to be revealed to those who choose to affiliate their lives with God's word.

> *'At that time Jesus answered and said, I thank thee O Father, Lord of heaven and earth, because thou hast hid these things from the wise and prudent, and hast revealed them unto babes.'* (Matthew 11:25)

When we speak in tongues we are expounding and exposing the deep things of God.

> '*But as it is written, Eye hath not seen, nor ear heard, neither have entered into the heart of man, the things which God hath prepared for them that love him. But God hath revealed them to us by his spirit: for the spirit searcheth all things, yea, the deep things of God.*'
>
> (1 Corinthians 2:9–10)

3. Direct Access to God

The Bible says:

> '*He that speaketh in an unknown tongue speaketh not unto men, but unto God: for no man understandeth him, howbeit in the spirit he speaketh mysteries.*' (1 Corinthians 14:2)

This is a revelation of the focus of the speaker's prayer. This keeps your prayer beyond the level of interruption, above satanic interference and influences. We are acquainted with the things happening in the spiritual realm when we pray or wait on the Lord.

Daniel had such an experience; he was taken into the spiritual realm where he realised that the Prince of Persia withheld the answer to his prayer. The devil must have been threatened by what Daniel asked of the Lord. The prayer of Daniel was granted the day he began to pray, but was interfered with for twenty-one days.

Many times Satan interferes with the secrets of our life, and is able to interfere with the answers to our prayer. This is because Satan hates the pouring out of new dreams which the Holy Spirit supplies into our hearts, when we pray. If we do not pray in tongues we lack, because we have been praying and pouring out new dreams which the Holy Spirit supplies into our hearts. By praying in tongues we declare the mysteries of God into our circumstances and the future.

Have you noticed that soon after you announce your intention to fast, renew your spiritual life, or raise your prayer life you face the greatest spiritual and carnal oppositions? This is because your intention and decisions were spoken out in an understandable language.

So your intentions have been opposed by the devil. This leaves the believer with no other option but to switch to a better 'frequency', speaking with other tongues!

> *'Praying always with all prayer and supplication in the spirit, and watching thereunto with all perseverance and supplication for all saints.'*
> (Ephesians 6:18)

> '*For what man knoweth the things of a man, save the spirit of man which is in him? even so the things of God knoweth no man, but the Spirit of God.*' (1 Corinthians 2:11)

4. Cutting Off Human Understanding

Speaking in Tongues, cuts off or by-passes our human understanding. This is contained in the scripture below:

> '*For if I pray in an unknown tongue, my spirit prayeth, but my understanding is unfruitful.*'
> (1 Corinthians 14:14)

The human mind processes information that is passed through it. If the information which comes in at a particular time does not conform to the standard it has established, it will be questioned or doubted.

So when we pray in tongues, we are offering a higher kind of prayer. The prayer is above the perception or processes of the human mind. Any prayer which is devoid of human understanding cannot be contaminated by sin, unbelief or doubt. The Bible says

> '*a double minded man is unstable in all his ways.*' (James 1:8)

Such a person would not receive anything from the Lord.

> *'For let not that man think that he shall receive anything of the Lord.'*   (James 1:7)

The greatest single factor that can cause God's blessings to elude believers is unbelief. Therefore as a Christian prays in tongues he does not doubt; after all who can know what is in a man

> *'except the spirit that is in him'?*
>   (1 Corinthians 2:11)

Praying in the spirit helps the believer pray unto an omnipotent God, who has no limitation. It is often difficult for the human mind to understand the greatness of God, and not to limit God's power. This is because the individual is constantly subject to the influences and the five senses.

But as we pray in tongues, we cannot limit God. We cannot limit what we have asked Him to do, neither can we limit the result of such praying, which ends up being

> *'exceeding abundantly above all that we ask or think, according to the power that worketh in us.'*   (Ephesians 3:20)

15

Once human understanding of our prayer is cut off, the problem of wandering thoughts does not arise. This does not suggest that an individual does not face the pressure to wander in his thought. The difference is that the prayer cannot be stopped by what one sees while praying or afterwards.

5. Praying in the Spirit

> *'For if I pray in an unknown tongue my spirit prayeth, but my understanding is unfruitful.'*
> (1 Corinthians 4:14)

> *'But ye, beloved, building up yourself on your most holy faith, praying in the Holy Ghost.'*
> (Jude 20)

> *'Likewise the spirit also helpeth our infirmities: for we know not what we should pray for as we ought: but the spirit itself maketh intercession for us with groanings which cannot be uttered.'*
> (Romans 8:26)

> *'I was in the spirit on the Lord's day...'*
> (Revelation 1:10)

Speaking in tongues helps to focus our praying, and helps to keep it within the realm of the supernatural. The importance of speaking in tongues as an approach to praying comes into focus as we realise that, when we pray in the Spirit, we cannot ask wrongly.

The Bible says:

> '*Ye ask, and receive not because ye ask amiss, that ye may consume it upon your lusts.*'
>
> (James 4:3)

We ask wrongly for things because of our intention to use them to fulfil carnal desires. When we pray in tongues such ungodly intentions are divorced from our desires.

6. Singing in the Spirit

Just as it is possible to sing in other languages, so it is with tongues. The Bible says:

> '*I will sing with the spirit.*'
>
> (1 Corinthians 14:15)

God has given us a beautiful language by which we can sing His praise, or make requests. Some of the songs we sing in known languages are songs of petition or consecration e.g.

> 'Abba, Father, let me be yours and yours alone.
> May my will forever be, ever more your own.'

17

I am convinced that as we sing in tongues during the periods in which we are praying for things or dedicating our lives or something else, we are expressing it in its highest form, though in song.

Exhortation, edification or messages of comfort could also come across in 'singing in tongues',

> *'Speaking to yourselves in psalms and hymns and spiritual songs, singing and making melody in your heart to the Lord.'*　(Ephesians 5:19)

Singing in tongues will expose your spirit to a higher form of praise; it will call your heart to a higher form of worship and help you to spontaneously *'sing a new song unto the Lord'* as the scripture says.

7. Language of Thanksgiving and Worship

Speaking in tongues is the best way to give God the highest praise. The people who assembled in the house of Cornelius were challenged by Peter's message to make a commitment to God. They must have believed in the message which promised remission of sins because the next thing which followed was a powerful outpouring of the Holy Spirit. It resulted in the magnifying of God by the recipients.

Often-times when we are worshipping the Lord, we run short of words which should express worship. So we start to play with words and phrases as they come to mind. But this is not the situation when we worship in tongues.

When we worship in tongues we move away from the limitations of the human language to speak of the high praises of God. At that point there is no break in our communication process. Believers should activate the habit of praising the Lord in tongues for a substantial amount of time each day.

At congregational meetings tongues should be used, incorporated, and upheld as part of our worship. It is advisable as a corporate body to raise our voices higher in tongues while praying.

This was the context in which the singing with tongues or praising in tongues took place in the Scriptures. When the whole congregation is involved it gives God the highest praise and honour.

Lastly, corporate praise in tongues will encourage a new and/or shy Christian who has not been baptised with the Holy Ghost to desire the baptism of the Holy Spirit. Those who have the potential to speak in tongues fluently would be encouraged and quickened as well.

I attended a Signs and Wonders Conference at Westminster Central Hall, London, in 1984. A Chinese lady received the baptism of the Holy Ghost. Immediately she started speaking fluently in French. This lady never spoke French prior to this time!

The beauty of it was that she was speaking the

high praises of God, while describing and affirming the vision of God's glory.

8. Spiritual Refreshment

One Mr Ebenezer and his wife were members of our Congregation. He came to England to do a Doctorate Programme in some aspect of the Portuguese language. When Ebenezer started writing up his projects, he suffered an incredible mental block. This had never happened to him before. His project was below standard; in his desperate condition he came to me for counselling.

The best possible counsel I could give him was to spend a substantial amount of time praying in tongues before he started work every day. He followed my advice and it worked. The blockage cleared, he became as mentally alert as he used to be!

Through our daily activities we become tired both mentally, physically and spiritually. Such tiredness is not relieved through mere rest.

Elijah was fatigued and sat under the juniper tree until an angel of the Lord fed him. Then he went in the strength of that food for forty days. It is possible to exhaust all our spiritual strength by not taking time away from our busy schedule to rest and pray. However, as the believer spends time worshipping in tongues he will find a lightness in his spirit.

This refreshment is not just for the exhausted but also for people who are jaded. Some people get home on particular days too exhausted to spend any appreciable time in prayer before going to bed, yet not wanting to go to sleep without praying. As you take a little time to worship and pray in tongues you will find that as the scriptures indicate:

> '*he maketh intercession for the saints according to the will of God.*'　　　　　(Romans 8:27)

> '*To whom he said, This is the rest wherewith ye may cause the weary to rest; and this is the refreshing: yet they would not hear.*'
> 　　　　　　　　　　　　　　(Isaiah 28:12)

I remember preaching in Christ Chapel Lagos (one of the fastest growing churches in Nigeria). Two hours before this vital ministry I burned out the clutch of the car as I was driving around town. I could not move the car away and needed to get home before going to the church. The pressure of a breakdown, the hassle of getting a taxi on time in such a tough city, and the fact that time was running out began to weigh me down. The only thing I could do was to worship in tongues in the taxi, the bathroom and throughout this ordeal. When I got to the church I experienced a wonderful outflow of the Word with a mighty anointing. Great testimonies accompanied us on that day.

This is not an excuse for prayerless or shoddy ministering, but a true and objective response to occasions when we need to draw on an ability which resides in us as a potential power to be released into our situations.

9. It is a Way of Full Surrender

One profound reason why speaking in tongues is necessary is because of the effect it has on the vocal chords. It is not difficult to yield many areas of our life to God, our jobs, our homes, ambitions, desires, dreams and trivial pursuits. However while it is easy to submit these aspects of our lives, it is hard to discipline the tongue, which is a very small member of the body.

> '*Even so the tongue is a little member, and boasteth great things. Behold how great a matter a little fire kindleth! And the tongue is a fire, a world of iniquity: so is the tongue among our members, that it defileth the whole body, and setteth on fire the course of nature.*'
>
> (James 3:5, 6)

There is hardly a believer who has not at one time struggled to keep their tongue under control. We all have, at some point, used our tongue wrongly to hurt or make other people unhappy. But as believers learn to occupy what seems to be idle times with speaking in tongues, the temptation to use their tongue in negative circumstances reduces.

(a) The believer will be tempted to drift into deceitful flattery.

> '*He who rebuketh a man will afterward find more favour than he who flattereth with the tongue.*' (Proverbs 28:23)

(b) There will be the pressure to participate in corridor gossip and slander.

> '*A naughty person, a wicked man, walketh with a froward mouth.*'

> '*Frowardness is in his heart, he deviseth mischief continually; he soweth discord.*'
> (Proverbs 6:12, 14)

Gossip is a false exaggerated report maliciously discussed and circulated about a person. It goes without saying that God abhors gossips and men find it difficult to trust a gossip with sensitive information. Surrendering this failure to God and constantly speaking in tongues will transform the believer and bring discipline to his speech life.

Furthermore the believer's constant flow in tongues will block out arguments, striving, angry words, boasting and foolish jesting, that is talk that is not edifying, silly, useless, foul and profane.

> *'Let no corrupt communication proceed out of your mouth, but that which is good to the use of edifying, that it may minister grace unto the hearers.'*　　　　　(Ephesians 4:29)

> *'Neither filthiness, nor foolish talking, nor jesting, which are not convenient: but rather giving of thanks.'*　　　　　(Ephesians 5:4)

He will not have time for verbosity. One who is verbose usually feels compelled to give his comments, even though in his much saying he says things of microscopic substance. But as the believer constantly speaks in his heavenly language, he will find that

> *'in quietness and confidence shall be your strength.'*　　　　　(Isaiah 30:15)

This is not suggesting that people who speak in tongues have overcome the problem of negative communication and can control their tongue. However this book is all about learning to exercise all the power of heaven and earth to bless, to conquer, deliver, and heal, as the case may be. The exercise of such power is facilitated through tongues.

The more you surrender your tongue for the use of the Holy Spirit, the less you participate in mundane and fruitless communication; also the easier it is for the Holy Spirit to help discipline our tongues.

10. Shutting Yourself Off From the World

There is a constant need to keep 'far from the madding crowd'. God does not want us to cut ourselves off completely from wicked, vicious men because we have to witness to them. Rather God warns us not to love,

> '*the world, neither the things that are in the world. If any man love the world, the love of the Father is not in him.*' (1 John 2:15)

This instruction is necessary because of the numerous attractions that can divert the attention of the believer. There are many ways to protect yourself from the influence of the world. One of them is learning to apply the principle of

> '*Praying without ceasing.*'
> (2 Thessalonians 5:17)

It is difficult to conceive of any other way to pray continuously other than in tongues. It would be like travelling on a long boring journey, or sitting in a committee meeting with little or no interest.

During visits to some offices, while killing time, one is left with glossy but dry magazines to browse through. At such times the believer could occupy himself praying in tongues silently or imperceptibly.

Another situation which demands protecting your spirit from the world and speaking in tongues is illustrated by one lady's experience. Angela had applied for a job which was several steps above the one she was engaged in, although within the same department. She studied hard in preparation for this interview, as she knew the areas the questions would be based on. But things went contrary to her expectation. Before Angela went for this interview, I advised her to pray in tongues, as this would build her confidence and remove doubt and fear. Angela would not heed the advice. She thought it was better if she prayed in the language she understood to ensure that she prayed for her desires. As she approached the venue of the interview, a heavy spirit of fear came upon her, shattering her confidence. She lost control and blanked out in a fearful way. The Bible identifies this kind of fear as a spirit.

> *'For God hath not given us the spirit of fear but of power, and of love, and of a sound mind.'*
> (2 Timothy 1:7)

The only way to guard against this kind of fear is to constantly pray in tongues. Such blockages are demonic attacks.

Consistency in praying in tongues is a weapon the believer should use when it is difficult to overcome worry and tension in difficult times, and when it seems difficult to deal with the defying situation. Examples include emotional states which sometimes have control over the mind. Paul cautions the believer to overcome them positively when he said:

> *'Be careful for nothing; but in everything by prayer and supplication with thanksgiving let your requests be made known unto God.'*
> (Philippians 4:6)

Keeping oneself from the world is also necessary because of the danger of a wandering heart.

> *'Keep thy heart with all diligence; for out of it are the issues of life.'*   (Proverbs 4:23)

The Christian who spends hours watching television cannot expect to develop the language of 'familiarity' with the throne of God. Jesus said:

> *'for out of the abundance of the heart the mouth speaketh.'*   (Matthew 12:34b)

The best discipline one can give his heart therefore is to bring it under control by focusing on the language of the Spirit to build the inner man.

11. Learning to Avoid Doubt

Doubt is the greatest thief of all God's spiritual blessings to man. While faith is acting on the Word of God, doubt is the opposite and is like saying God does not mean what He says.

The fives senses do not affirm faith but promote doubt. They are the tools by which we relate to the world around us. Since the law of faith is different, the five senses tend to make us regard spiritual things as irrational. The problem of doubt is complicated by the weakness of the natural languages by which we make our requests known to the Father.

The things doubt can do to our prayer are indicated in the message below:

> 'For verily I say unto you, that whosoever shall say unto this mountain, be thou removed and be thou cast into the sea; and shall not doubt in his heart, but shall believe that those things which he saith shall come to pass; he shall have whatsoever he saith.' (Mark 11:23)

This was said by Jesus.

Doubt can stand between the believer and his victory. On the contrary, as the believer prays in tongues, his mental processes (which conflict with spiritual reality) are rendered inactive.

You can only discredit a statement made in the language you understand. Tongues protects our prayer, so that it is not aborted prematurely before fruition through unbelief. This means that where the believer is having a problem submitting his desires to God, as he or she speaks in tongues, the will of God is established. The Spirit of God in the believer will pray rightly when his human spirit does otherwise.

12. The Believer's War-Cry

> *'For though we walk in the flesh we do not war after the flesh: For the weapons of our warfare are not carnal, but mighty through God to the pulling down of strong holds: Casting down imaginations, and every high thing that exalteth itself against the knowledge of God, and bringing into captivity every thought to the obedience of Christ.'*　　(2 Corinthians 10:3–5)

The reality of spiritual warfare comes upon the believer as he grows in the grace of the Lord Jesus Christ. It does not take him too long in the faith to discover that whoever receives Christ will also experience a powerful encounter from the kingdom of the devil. One of the spheres of these attacks is the believer's mind. Images could easily be built of failures, disappointments, set-backs, business failures and even the thought of backsliding.

One of the devil's favourite weapons is to raise questions about the wisdom of God. Satan likes to belittle whatever God says:

> *'And the serpent said to the woman you shall not surely die! For God knows that in the day*

29

*you eat from it your eyes will be opened, and
you will be like God, knowing good and evil.'*
(Genesis 3:4–5)

Before the devil's lie sticks and affects the
believer's faith, he should cry out in the language of
heaven to the One who has instructed that such a
cry should come to Him:

*'I the Lord am your God, who brought you up
from the land of Egypt; open your mouth and I
will fill it.'*
(Psalm 87:10)

Thieves who come to steal, kill, and destroy are
usually the violent types not ordinary pick-pockets.
The devil is more than a pick-pocket, rather a
malevolent being, therefore should be dealt with
violently. Deal with any attack by praying in
tongues for a considerable length of time. As you
make this a habit the Holy Spirit prays against the
attack through you.

*'And in the same way the spirit also helps our
weakness; for we do not know how to pray as
we should, but the spirit himself intercedes for
us with groanings too deep for words.*

*He who searches the hearts knows what the
mind of the spirit is, because he intercedes for
the saints according to the will of God.'*
(Romans 8:26–27)

Chapter 2

How to Receive the Gifts of the Holy Spirit

I was invited to minister on the gifts of the Holy Spirit on a Sunday in 1979. My hosts were a group of young people from a Baptist Church. The group met frequently to study the scriptures on the Holy Spirit. This church did not believe in the operation of the Holy Spirit and his gifts in individuals. Many people turned out for this meeting out of curiosity. This little classroom where the meeting took place was crowded and over forty adults attended the meeting.

After sharing on the need for the Holy Spirit, I prayed briefly for them to receive the gift. Then I simply urged them to 'receive the Holy Spirit'. I did not lay hands on any of them; all of them received the Holy Spirit and started speaking in tongues.

That year I also conducted a Holy Ghost service

for the Student Christian Movement of the University in the same city, and ministered in some churches. On most occasions I did lay on hands. The truth is that the Holy Spirit can be received with or without the laying on of hands. But there are some basic steps the recipient might have to take in order to receive the Holy Spirit.

1. Aspiration

Jesus said:

> *'Blessed are they which do hunger and thirst after righteousness: For they shall be filled.'*
>
> (Matthew 5:6)

A strong desire to receive the Holy Spirit is absolutely essential.

The desire must be for the right motive. Simon, the sorcerer, had the wrong motive for seeking the Holy Spirit. He probably saw the experience from a business point of view, therefore he thought it would be a good investment.

> *'And when Simon saw that through the laying on of the Apostles hands the Holy Ghost was given, he offered them money, Saying, "Give me also this power, that on whomsoever I lay hands, he may receive the Holy Ghost".'*
>
> (Acts 8:18–19)

Our quest to receive must be because of the power Jesus said the Holy Spirit will impart when he comes, so that we can be effective witnesses.

> *'And ye shall be witnesses unto me both in Jerusalem, and in all Judea, and in Samaria, and unto the uttermost part of the earth.'*
>
> (Acts 1:8)

The lack of honest desire to use the gifts of the Holy Spirit perhaps accounts for the reasons why he is such a latent resident of many hearts. This is the reason people live in despair and walk in defeat, even after receiving the Holy Spirit.

The believer needs power and authority in his life. Authority will help you to take charge over circumstances.

> *'And these signs shall follow them that believe; In my name they shall cast out devils; they shall speak with new tongues; They shall take up serpents; and if they drink any deadly thing, it shall not hurt them; they shall lay hands on the sick, and they shall recover.'* (Mark 16:17, 18)

A police constable can stop anybody or call any time on the grounds of reasonable suspicion. Such a constable would be acting on the authority vested on him by the State. Power in the New Testament is from the Greek word '*dunamis*' from which are derived the words 'dynamite' or 'dynamic'.

2. Believing

> '*If ye then being evil, know how to give goods gifts unto your children, how much more shall your father which is in heaven give good things to them that ask him?*'　　　(Matthew 7:11)

Believing as a next step has to do with receiving the Holy Spirit by faith. You must believe that the gift is for you and that God will give it to you the moment you express the desire for it. Faith is absolutely necessary to receive the Holy Spirit and to subsequently manifest his gifts. It has been established that faith is acting on the Word of God. Receiving the Holy Spirit is a promise of God; once your desire is of God, it will be honoured.

> '*Then Peter said unto them, Repent, and be Baptised every one of you in the name of Jesus Christ for the remission of sins, and ye shall receive the gift of the Holy Ghost.*'

(Acts 2:38)

Faith will give you a sense of expectation. Many things happen because we expect them to happen in a certain way. They happen because we believe strongly that it will be so. You must exercise your faith strongly as you prepare to receive the Holy Spirit.

3. Confession

The Bible describes Jesus as the Apostle and High Priest of our confession.

> *'Wherefore, holy brethren, partakers of the heavenly calling, consider the Apostle and High Priest of our profession, Christ Jesus.'*
>
> (Hebrews 3:1)

This suggests that Jesus takes our prayers, praises and confessions to the Father, and brings back the result of our desire.

Since we have an audience with Jesus, the confession of the person who seeks to receive the Holy Spirit should be right. It is very easy to receive the Holy Spirit but you must overcome unbelief, doubts, fears and false doctrines.

Firstly, let it be clear in your mind that you do not need to tarry for the Holy Spirit. In all the five instances where people received the Holy Spirit in the book of Acts only on the first occasion did they have to wait. This was the first outpouring on the Church. The specific day of the first outpouring (Pentecost) had been chosen. Jesus instructed his disciples to gather in Jerusalem to receive the power.

> *'not many days hence.'* (Acts 1:5)

He was not laying down waiting as a condition for receiving the Holy Spirit.

> *'And, behold, I send the promise of my Father upon you: but tarry ye in the city of Jerusalem, until ye be endued with power from on high.'*
> (Luke 24:49)

> *'And, being assembled together commanded them that they should not depart from Jerusalem, but wait for the promise of the Father, which, saith he, ye have heard of me. For John truly baptised with the Holy Ghost not many days hence.'* (Acts 1:4, 5)

Secondly, you do not have to pray 'the prayer of petition' before the Lord to receive the Holy Spirit. The Bible makes it clear the Holy Spirit is a gift.

> *'Then Peter said unto them, repent and be baptised every one of you in the name of Jesus Christ for the remission of sins, and ye shall receive the gift of the Holy Ghost. For the promise is unto you, and to your children, and*

> *to all afar off, even as many as the Lord our*
> *God shall call.'*   (Acts 2:38, 39)

This establishes the fact that Holy Spirit baptism is a gift to any member of the Body of Christ. Petitioning God for a promise, or rather begging the person who promised you a gift, is not exactly the best step to receiving the promise made. Whatever step you take should affirm your faith and your understanding of God's word and His way.

To receive the Holy Spirit first,

> *'enter his gates with thanksgiving, and go into*
> *his courts with praise: be thankful unto him*
> *and bless his name.'*   (Psalm 100:4)

Start with the high praises of God, lifting Him high above the heavens for who He is. Lift Him up as King of Kings and Lord of Lords.

He draws you unto Himself. You will be able to recount all the goodness of God in your life and His wondrous love to you. Then thank Him for the gift of the Holy Spirit which He promised to give you. Maintain an attitude of thanksgiving and praise for at least five minutes. Stop at a point and start to say or sing 'Alleluia.'

This word is suggested purely because all through Scripture the only word which is of praise and has heavenly origin is 'Alleluia'.

> '*And after these things I heard a great voice of much people in heaven, saying, Alleluia; Salvation, and glory, and honour, and power, unto the Lord our God.*'   (Revelation 19:1)

Also in the same chapter the Bible says,

> '*And the four and twenty elders and the four beasts fell down and worshipped God that sat on the throne, saying, Amen; Alleluia.*'

> '*And I heard as it were the voice of a great multitude, and as the voice of many waters, and as the voice of mighty thunderings, saying, Alleluia: for the Lord God omnipotent reigneth.*'   (Revelation 19:4, 6)

Now let me suggest a very practical exercise of faith which has helped many: At some point stop saying or singing Alleluia and by faith speak forth anything which comes through your mouth. It may appear to sound like babbling or real words which seem to sound meaningless.

Do not stop until you gain confidence in your spirit to continue to speak freely.

Chapter 3

Types of Tongues

Many times I meet believers who were once baptised with the Holy Spirit but have lost the language immediately or shortly after the experience. Many are not sure if they should seek for the Baptism of the Holy Spirit afresh, or just pray to speak in tongues again.

This confusion arises because many do not know that the first time one receives the Baptism of the Holy Spirit and speaks in tongues, that experience is often called an 'INITIAL EVIDENCE'. This is so designated because of the five instances where people received the Holy Spirit in the scriptures, (Acts 2:4, 8:17–18; 10:44–46; 9:17; 19:6).

The gift which accompanied on three of the five occasions where specific gifts were involved was speaking in tongues. On one occasion it was recorded that they spoke in tongues and prophesied:

> *'And when Paul had laid his hands upon them, the Holy Ghost came on them; and they spake with tongues and prophesied.'*   (Acts 19:6)

When you receive the Holy Spirit you may speak in tongues and prophesy for a few weeks. This serves as an initial evidence that you have received the Baptism of the Holy Spirit.

People lose the language of the Holy Spirit if they do not enjoy it regularly while praying. The believer needs to move from the 'initial evidence' to every day, by faith, trusting that he will move on to use tongues devotionally.

Much of what has been written as reasons for speaking in tongues relates to this second stage. But just as a newly acquired human language will not flow without practice, it will be difficult to go straight away from the 'initial evidence' to a 'LANGUAGE OF DEVOTION'.

The third dimension is when it serves as a MINISTRY gift in public. It is only in this dimension, that control is brought to speaking in tongues. The necessity for such control is clear; to allow the message to minister to the listeners as the tongue is accompanied by an interpretation.

> *'Therefore, the person who speaks in an (unknown) tongue should pray (for the power) to interpret and explain what he says.'*
>
> (1 Corinthians 14:13, Amplified)

Those speaking in tongues loudly in the open meeting must be able to interpret according to this verse. There may have been gifts of other tongues too. Messages should come from only two to three at one time and there should be an interpretation. If there is no interpretation, the person or persons speaking in tongues in public should keep silent, according to Paul.

> *'If some speak in a (strange) tongue, let the number be limited to two or at most three, and each one, (taking his) turn, and let one interpret and explain (what is said). But if there is no one to do the interpreting, let each of them keep still in church and talk to himself and to God.'*
>
> (1 Corinthians 14:27–28, Amplified)

The result of such an interpreted message on the believer is revelation of his sinfulness, the reproving he gets for it, the subsequent conviction in his heart, and on many occasions, the Holy Spirit lays the secrets of his heart bare.

There are people who think the gift of interpretation can be used in private to understand what they have said in tongues or to get a response from the Lord. The context in which the gift of interpretation is mentioned is only in open Body ministry.

Chapter 4

The Operation of Tongues

1. Do It Regularly

The importance of speaking in tongues has been enumerated in the first chapter. Speaking in tongues builds our human spirit up and introduces our spirit to the secret things of God. These advantages should motivate one to practise it regularly. Spend much of your time of personal devotion and prayer speaking in tongues. Make it your 'tool' for praying without ceasing.

There should be times when you pray in tongues for two hours or more if possible.

2. Do Not Listen to Lying Spirits

The human mind is often exposed to doubts and questions whenever it has to handle supernatural things. Do not be surprised if you are caught in the web of doubting the language of the spirit you are speaking.

Dr Howard Courtney* said in 1979, 'Fifty years after receiving the Holy Spirit, the devil still tells me that I have not received the Holy Ghost and what I am speaking is not of God'. You will be tempted to raise questions whether what you are speaking is genuine or not, because your human mind may simply disagree with what comes out verbally. It might therefore classify it as false. The question of falsehood does not arise if you were born again when you prayed for this experience. You cannot ask for the Holy Spirit and receive something else.

> '*Or what man is there of you, whom if his son ask bread, will he give him a stone?*'
>
> (Matthew 7:9)

Lying spirits will want to intimidate you so that you can stop speaking in tongues. The reason is because of the harm it does to the kingdom of darkness. Lying spirits will attempt to put you under pressure so that you raise objections and question your personal experience.

You have to positively affirm what you have

---

* A one time member of the Advisory Board of the Pentecostal World Conference and Pastor of the Angelus Temple (the Headquarters Church of the Foursquare Gospel).

received. There may be one in a thousand false experiences, but we should not do away with true experiences because of some falsehoods.

3. Keep Your Heart Right

> '*Keep and guard your heart with all vigilance and above all that you guard, for out of it flow the springs of life.*'
>
> (Proverbs 4:23, Amplified)

The things you accommodate in your heart could affect the flow of spiritual awareness, for good or bad.

Hearts that are filled with bitterness, anger and unforgiveness cannot be the breeding ground of spiritual creativity. Such hearts cannot be drawn to the ways of God.

Keep your heart. If the enemy cannot steal your joy, ruin your peace, or sow the wrong seed in your heart, you are guaranteed to have a great time in the things of the Spirit.

4. Do Not Submit to Objections

There are millions of born-again Christians who have not received the Baptism of the Holy Spirit, or even subscribe to the possibility of the experience. Sadly they are often the most vehement voice against the experience. Their objections to the experience vary. Some of them believe the whole Church has received the Baptism of the Holy Spirit because of the day of Pentecost. They support their belief with 1 Corinthians 12:13.

> *'For by one Spirit are we all baptised into one body, whether we be Jews or Gentiles, whether we be bond or free; and have been all made to drink into one spirit.'*

On the other hand, there are Evangelicals who want the Spirit but not the gifts. Russel Spittler puts it this way. 'Too many Evangelicals want the Spirit but not the gifts, an attitude that violates scriptural teachings:

> *'But eagerly desire the greater gifts.'*
>
> (1 Corinthians 12:31)

Chapter 5

The Historical Basis for Tongues

There have been paradigm shifts in the attitude of churches and society to the experience of speaking in tongues and to those who speak in tongues. When modern Pentecostalism started in 1906, after it had generally ceased from the Church (though not totally), the attitude was one of **RESISTANCE**. Pentecostals were avoided, and sometimes excluded from programmes which brought believers together. This attitude generally continued until the end of the Second World War.

The explosive growth of Pentecostal denominations, the rise of great Pentecostal evangelists like Aimee Semple McPherson – whose ministry was from 1923 to 1944, Oral Roberts, who built a university, the Jeffrey Brothers in England, who founded Elim, and John Lake, who held the first non-segregated meetings in South Africa, and many others moved the shift from resistance to **TOLERANCE**.

Further tolerance came with the advent of modern evangelists like Billy Graham. One of his approaches to crusades is to insist on the co-operation of all the churches in a city, which leaves main-line churches with no choice but to co-operate with Pentecostals.

Movement from tolerance to **ACCEPTANCE** came with the efforts of men like David Du Plessis, the late South African elder statesman who virtually travelled round the world, convincing Pastors, Bishops, etc. of the large Protestant denominations to see the need for Pentecostal experience.

His efforts yielded the conversion of men like Dennis Bennett of the Episcopalian Church and began what became known as Neo-Pentecostalism. Neo-Pentecostals were men who of necessity belonged to the High Churches, i.e. Lutheran, Episcopalian, (American Anglican) Methodist, but had received the Baptism of the Holy Spirit.

Today there are over 400 million people who speak in tongues around the world. What started in 1906 in a small prayer meeting, where William Seymour, a black preacher, first spoke in tongues has become a world-wide phenomenon. It can be safely said that attitudes have since changed from the experience being that of acceptance to **SUBSTANCE**.

Ministering salvation, healing, and especially the

reception of the gift of the Holy Spirit, has been the focal point of the Full Gospel Businessman's Fellowship International. This is one group which has translated glossolalia (tongue speaking) to a gift and experience for the rich, famous, intellectuals, rulers, as well as the ruled. They have reached all classes of men with the message of the Full Gospel.

After the Neo-Pentecostalists, there have been, and still are, the Charismatics. These are believers who believe in the gifts of the Holy Spirit, but do not necessarily belong to any of the large denominations.

There are many local churches which belong to denominations which do not subscribe to the separate infilling of the Holy Spirit and the gift of tongues.

It is encouraging to realise that there is a mighty outpouring of the gift of the Holy Ghost and speaking in tongues in places like South America and Asia. In Africa about ninety-five per cent of born-again Christians speak in tongues. Until recently, most of Latin and Central America was ninety-five per cent Roman Catholic. In these recent times there has been a mighty outpouring of the Holy Spirit on these continents. It is the in-thing to be baptised with the Holy Spirit.

The second largest church in the world (in Chile) with over two hundred and fifty thousand members is a Pentecostal church (the Jolabeche Church in Santiago).

The same wave of the Spirit is going on in Asia. In Asia the power of God is confronting and confounding oriental beliefs, gods and philosophies. Dr Yongi Cho's church in Seoul, Korea, exceeds half a million people. It is a church in the heart of Asia, very much involved in binding the spirit of rebellion and repression, which goes on in Seoul, Korea. Internationally it has touched the world by its teachings on the principles of church growth and the cell unit system.

Some have insisted that the gift of speaking in tongues ceased with the Apostles. They think the experience cannot occur in these contemporary times. This is certainly a lie out of the pit of hell. This lie is used to question the experience and lose the blessing which follows the practice.

In the next pages I will try to establish the fact that the gift of tongues was in manifestation even during the dark ages of the Church.

Patristic Period 100–500 AD

One of the Early Church Fathers, Polycarp, who was said to be a disciple of John the Apostle and Bishop of Smyrna, was martyred in AD 155. In his prayer at his martyrdom which was recorded by Marcion, from an eye witness account a year later, he appears to have prayed in tongues.

About the same time Irenaeus, the Bishop of Lyons, wrote in *Against Heresies* 'In like manner we do also hear many brethren in the church who possess prophetic gifts, and who through the Spirit speak all kinds of languages.'

Tertullian, one of the early Church fathers, encouraged believers of his time to speak in tongues. He wrote, 'Let him produce a Psalm, a vision, a prayer, whenever an interpretation of tongues occurs to him.'

In the third century Novatian of Rome wrote concerning the Holy Spirit, 'This is he who places prophets, in the Church, instructs teachers, directs tongues.'

The fourth and fifth centuries had men like John Chrysostum, Bishop of Constantinople, who asserted that speaking in tongues, 'Now no longer takes place.'

This was followed in the same Fifth Century by Augustine's down-grading of tongues in his *Confessions*. But twenty years later he wrote in *City of God*, 'Once I realised how many miracles were occurring in our own day and which were so like the miracles of old. It is only two years ago that the keeping of records was begun here in Hippo.'

Furthermore, men like Hilary, Bishop of Poitiers, Ambrose, Bishop of Milan, and the Egyptian Abbot Pachomius all spoke in tongues. Ambrose and Pachomius clearly showed how this gift was manifesting in their locality.

During the same period which John Chrysostum said tongues, 'Now no longer takes place', Ambrose the Bishop said in his writing,

'The Holy Spirit,' that 'Behold the Father established the teachers; Christ also established them in churches; and just as the Father gives the grace of healings, so the Son also has bestowed it.'

The Medieval Period 600–1500

This period in the history of the Church was a in sense anachronistic. On one hand the Church was very low in the manifestation of the Spirit and his gifts, on the other the Church was powerful because it controlled the politics of this period. The Church made and deposed kings.

There is no clear record that tongue speaking was practised during the Sixth to Twelfth centuries in the West. The gift was in constant use though, in the Eastern Church.

Many within the Greek Orthodox Church, including the Patriarch of Constantinople, maintained that the gift never ceased among their monastic orders. According to the Encyclopaedia Britannica, by the Thirteenth Century Western Mendicant Friars prayed in tongues.

During the Fifteenth to the Seventeenth centuries, two of the saints canonised, St Francis Xavier and St Lewis Bertrand, had the gift of tongues listed among the reasons for their being honoured.

The purposes of this book is not to argue against the canonisation of saints but only refers to the event for the primary purpose it serves.

Reformation Period

There is some evidence that Martin Luther received the gift of tongues before his final monastic vows. St Teresa of Avila spoke in tongues regularly and her reference to it in her autobiography remains one of the loveliest description of tongues:

> 'I do not know any other terms for describing it or explaining it. Nor does the soul then know what to do, whether to speak or to be silent, whether to laugh or to weep. This prayer is a glorious foolishness, a heavenly madness where the true wisdom is learned; and it is for the soul a most delightful way of enjoying.'

The French Calvinists (Huguenots) had the gift of tongues operating regularly in their midst. It culminated in an extraordinary incident at the beginning of the Eighteenth Century when more than three hundred children prophesied and spoke in tongues with astonishing power and accuracy.

Next were the Quakers (The Society of Friends) who reached great heights in the manifestation of spiritual gifts.

Their literature records visions, healing, prophecies and a power which they likened to Pentecost. One specific reference shows it:

'We received often the pouring down of the Spirit upon us, and our mouths opened, and we spake with new tongues as the Lord gave utterance.'

The Modern Period 1700 Onwards

I would like to group the people who lived from the Eighteenth century under modern Pentecostal experience, because some of today's denominations, and some of today's ministers had a beginning which is directly or indirectly related to this period.

The Methodist revival broke out during this century, and although their history seems clouded with the things historians chose to emphasise, there was a lot of manifestation of the gift of tongues in their midst. Thomas Walsh, one of the associates of John Wesley entered in his diary on the 8th of March 1750:

'This morning the Lord gave me a language I know not of, raising my soul to Him in a wondrous manner.'

The Moravian Brethren, a ministry with world-wide missionary zeal, and whose lives of piety had a profound effect on John Wesley and his ministry, also spoke in tongues.

An anonymous critic of the Moravian Brethren penned a statement which was meant to denunciate tongues, but showed that the gift was operational in their midst. He wrote about them and their leader Count Zinzendorf,

'He and his followers were great in the Spirit and affected strange convulsive heavings and unnatural postures. In one of these fits they commonly broke into some disconnected jargon, which they often passed upon the vulgar as the exuberant and resistless evacuations of the Spirit and many other such enthusiastic stuff.'

The Nineteenth century revival of holiness laid a good foundation for the massive outpouring of the Spirit in the Twentieth Century. Tongues was in manifestation at this time, and people as diverse as Edward Irving of the Catholic Apostolic Church in London, to Pastor Blumhardt of Germany were ministering through tongues. The gift was poured out in countries as far apart from each other as Russia, Sweden, North America, France, Germany and India.

Towards the end of the Nineteenth Century, many holiness churches sprang up, and a mighty revival broke out in North America, but before the Holy Spirit outpouring in America, revival had broken out in Wales, in 1904. This resulted in the outpouring of the Holy Spirit, even if tongues was not reported as spoken.

Jessie Penn-Lewis wrote of the times by saying,

'Some men were so literally filled with the Spirit that others would have said, *"they are drunk with new wine."*'

Meanwhile in 1906 William Seymour, a graduate of Charles Parham's Bethel Bible College in Kansas, went back to Los Angeles with a strong desire to be filled with the Holy Spirit. One day while praying, Seymour received the Baptism of the Holy Spirit, and spoke in tongues. He began ministering the same experience to people who came from far and wide to receive the Holy Spirit. Very soon people were coming from all over the world and the Azusa Street Los Angeles revival fire touched all the continents of the world.

Today there is a conservative estimate of four hundred million people who speak in tongues around the world. Men and women came from all the states of America, and from far countries to witness the out-pouring of the Holy Spirit, at Azusa Street. These visitors went back to touch whole States, Nations, Churches and lives with the new experience.

The Church of God, Cleveland Tennessee, was virtually the first to take the experience to the West Indies, which spread rapidly on all the islands.

Latin America and Central America have had outpourings of the Holy Spirit with millions today being baptised in the Holy Spirit and speaking in tongues.

Prior to this outpouring, more than 96 per cent of this subcontinent were Roman Catholic, clearly because of the Spanish Conquest. Today, the second largest church in the world is on this continent and it is Pentecostal.

Africa

Probably ninety-eight per cent of born-again Africans speak in tongues today. The record might have been better if churches which emphasise the receiving of the Holy Spirit were encouraged to come with the colonisation of most countries.

In the cases where people read the scriptures, believed and went to practise it, the result was indigenous Pentecostal or Charismatic churches. Records were not kept during the early years.

In the Ivory Coast, one Prophet Harris, a Liberian from the Barbos tribe, started his ministry in 1913 after a remarkable revelation from God. Although he was not profound in his understanding of the Scriptures, God honoured his faithfulness. This prophet travelled across the west coast of Africa preaching the gospel. At the end of his message, he would invite people to kneel before the cross. Through simple prayer, demons were cast out, people received the Holy Spirit and sinners confessed their sins.

In Nigeria, Faith Tabernacle and The Apostolic Church movement seemed to pioneer churches of Pentecostal experience, and were started by Pentecostal Missionaries like Reverend S.G. Elton who came from the Apostolic Church of Great Britain. These were followed by the Precious Stone Church which remained almost unknown outside Lagos, and Christ Apostolic Church which is the largest in the whole of the nation.

The greatest growth experienced by the Pentecostal movement in Nigeria was after the civil war which ended in 1970. More than ninety-five per cent of the people who speak in tongue in Nigeria currently got born again and filled with the Holy Spirit after the Civil War.

Today the out-pouring of the Holy Spirit has spread from Angola to Zimbabwe. It has gone beyond the babbling of the poor to the sweet language in the mouth of Ambassadors. Many of the fast growing churches in Western Europe have a strong presence of African Charismatics and Pentecostals.

Other Books and Tapes
by the Author

1. **Take a Giant Leap**
   (How to motivate yourself for a
   successful Christian Life)   £3.50

2. **Warriors of Righteousness**
   (Occupy your place for the Battle of
   the End Times)   £4.95

3. **Keeping Your Dreams Alive**
   (How to fulfil your God-given vision)   £2.50

Tape Packs

1. **Living on the Edge of a Miracle**
   (2 tape pack)   £6.00

2. **Living Dangerously – the Lifestyle
   of the Kingdom of God**
   (3 tape pack)   £8.00

3. **The Beginning of the End**
   (4 tape pack)   £10.00

4. **Breaking New Grounds**
   (3 tape pack)   £8.00

5. **Standing Tall in Shifting Times**
   (4 tape pack)   £10.00

Contact Addresses

Mattyson Media
57 Maryland Road
Stratford
London E15 1JL
Telephone No: 081-534 5593

Mattyson Media
8 Tinu Atobajaye Street
Off Celestial Bus Stop
Isolo
Lagos
Nigeria

The Kingsway International Christian Centre
c/o 55a Barking Road
Canning Town
London E16 4HB
Telephone No: 071-473 4445/6